Want to Play?
Kids Talk About Friendliness

Written by
Pamela Hill Nettleton

Illustrated by
Amy Bailey Muehlenhardt

Thanks to our advisers for their expertise, research, and advice:

Stephanie Goerger Sandahl, M.A., Counseling
Lutheran Social Services of Minnesota, Fergus Falls, Minnesota

Susan Kesselring, M.A., Literacy Educator
Rosemount-Apple Valley-Eagan (Minnesota) School District

PICTURE WINDOW BOOKS
Minneapolis, Minnesota

Managing Editors: Bob Temple, Catherine Neitge
Creative Director: Terri Foley
Editors: Brenda Haugen, Christianne Jones
Editorial Adviser: Andrea Cascardi
Designer: Nathan Gassman
Page production: Picture Window Books
The illustrations in this book were rendered digitally.

Picture Window Books
5115 Excelsior Boulevard
Suite 232
Minneapolis, MN 55416
877-845-8392
www.picturewindowbooks.com

Printed in the United States of America.

Library of Congress Cataloging-in-Publication Data
Nettleton, Pamela Hill.
Want to play? : kids talk about friendliness / written by Pamela Hill Nettleton;
    illustrated by Amy Bailey Muehlenhardt.
p. cm. — (Kids talk)
Includes bibliographical references and index.
ISBN 1-4048-0623-7 (reinforced library binding : alk. paper)
1. Friendship—Miscellanea—Juvenile literature. I. Muehlenhardt, Amy Bailey, 1974–
    II. Title. III. Series.
BF575.F66N48 2004
158.2'5—dc22
                                                    2003028233

Dear Kyle,

Whoever had your book last year kept it neat for you, right? What if someone had spilled orange juice in your math book? The pages would be stuck together. Your homework would be all messed up from missing the problems printed on the juicy pages. Yuck!

Your teacher is showing you how to be considerate. It may seem stupid at first, but give it a try! Hey—you could even use really cool paper to cover your book. Then you can make your boring textbook look cool!

Tina

Hi everyone! My name is Tina Truly. "T" to my pals. "Teee-naaa!" to my dad when he trips on my backpack after I forget it on the stairs.

I'm 13 years old, and I'm in seventh grade at Meandering Middle School. I admit it—I love giving people advice. Josh, my big brother, says I'm just nosy. I say I'm helpful! Kids tell me their problems, and I tell them what to do next. If I can't think of something wise, I check with my experts—my stepmom, my dad, my mom, Josh, my teachers, and my best friend, Josie.

Speaking of friends, in today's column I'll be talking about friendliness. Being a good friend. Finding new friends. Letting your friends help you. All kinds of friendly stuff. So read on!

Sincerely,

Tina Truly

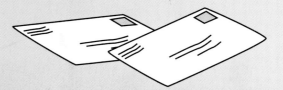

6

Dear Jamal,

I'm full of great ideas! That's why I like to give advice.

Nobody likes facing a classroom full of strangers. Yikes! It makes my hands sweat just thinking about it.

I remember a new kid who came to my school a couple of years ago. She walked into my classroom. The teacher told us her name. The new kid looked pretty scared. Then she smiled and said, "Hi. I hate being the new kid." We all laughed with her. That new kid became my best friend, Josie. I know Josie didn't want to leave her old house and her old friends, but I'm glad she did.

You could try making a joke like Josie did. I think it's easier to talk to people if you are laughing. Plus, you'll be the one to start talking. Kids will want to know more about you, but they might feel shy about asking. So say hello, and ask questions. Ask the guy sitting next to you if he plays baseball. Ask a kid on the bus if the school lunches are any good. Most kids just need help getting started. Then they'll talk. Like me—I'll talk and talk and talk.

Tina

Dear Tina,

I would like to be friends with one of the popular girls in school, but I'm not that cool. How can I do it?

Mandy

Dear Mandy,

I'll bet you're cooler than you think.

Let me tell you a story about being popular. Not long ago, I went to a party and saw school friends that I hadn't seen for years. Cynthia was the coolest girl in the entire school back then, but I never talked to her. She was popular, and I wasn't. I was too scared to talk to a popular kid.

The strangest thing happened at this party. Cynthia walked up to me and started talking. She said she never talked to me back at our old school because she thought I was too popular!

Me? Popular? Well, that's what Cynthia thought. She said I had lots of friends and seemed so smart. She didn't think I'd want another friend. I told her I thought she was the one with all the friends. We missed our chance at being friends because of things we imagined about each other.

So go ahead, and say hi to that popular girl. If you know you have something in common—like you both love playing soccer or you both take piano lessons—talk to her about that. She might be wishing that you would.

Tina

Dear Tina,

I am in **big** trouble! I had a fight with my friend MacKenzie. Not a little fight. A big fight. I even ripped her favorite poster. I can't believe I did that! Now MacKenzie is really mad at me, and I miss her as a friend. What can I do to be her friend again?

Emma

Dear Emma,

Friends do fight, but wrecking other people's stuff is never cool. Maybe you could use some of your money to buy MacKenzie a new poster. That would be a good start.

Tell MacKenzie you know you made a mistake, and you're sorry. If she's too mad to listen, give her a little more time to cool down. Wait a day or two, and then try that apology again. It doesn't have to be fancy. Try something like, "Hey, MacKenzie, I'm *so* sorry we got mad at each other, and I'm *really* sorry I ripped your poster."

Tell MacKenzie you miss hanging out with her. Let her know you want to be friends again. Promise that even if you're both mad, you'll try to talk it out. I'll bet MacKenzie is missing you, too, and might like it if you make the first move towards being friends again.

Tina

Dear Tina,

My sister says I'm not nice to my friends. She says I'm bossy and always have to have my own way. Maybe I am sometimes, but not all the time. Anyway, what's a good friend?

Olivia

Dear Olivia,

OK, let's try an experiment: Call up one of your friends and ask what's going on with her. Ask her what *she'd* like to do today. If she passes out in shock, then you know your sister wasn't just teasing you.

My friend Josie is a great listener. I can tell her all my problems, and she really listens to me. My buddy Kyle is a special friend because he can make me laugh until I cry. That guy is *so* funny! My big brother, Josh, is a pretty good friend, too. He gives me great advice. Yes, sometimes even *I* need advice!

What do all these friends have in common? We share our time together. When we hang out, we talk some about them and some about me. We do what they want sometimes, and what I want other times. We don't boss each other around.

Your sister might have a point. Since she is a sister, she might be making it sound worse than it really is just to bug you. Either way, it can't hurt to try to be more thoughtful and considerate of your friends for a while. She was trying to help—just like a good friend.

Tina

Dear Tina,

My mom says friends understand you when you are at your worst. My dad says my friends deserve my best behavior. Who is right?

Dylan

Dear Dylan,

If you ask me—and you did—both of your parents are right. They are each talking about a different part of friendship.

My brother once got really mad at himself after he missed a goal in a hockey game. He threw his stick and said a word that made my stepmom's eyebrows go up. Josh's coach made him sit out the rest of the game, and his team lost without him. His teammates were so mad at him. They wouldn't even talk to him after the game!

When we got home, Josh's friend Marty came over. Marty went straight up to Josh's room. I don't know what Marty said, but Josh was happy when he came downstairs. So your mom is right—a real friend is a friend even when things aren't perfect.

Your dad is right, too. My best friend always makes me feel special when I go to her house. She always gives me the biggest piece of pizza or cake. I get to sit in the best chair. She says I deserve it because I am her friend. I try to find ways to treat her special, too. I also do this for my other friends. Then when I screw up, they'll still be my true friends.

Tina

16

Dear Tina,

My friend Jessica says I can only have one best friend, but I have two: Jessica and Lori. When I play with Lori, Jessica gets mad. Am I doing something wrong?

Madison

Dear Madison,

You're not doing anything wrong! Jessica is just feeling jealous. Jealousy is a crummy feeling to have. It doesn't feel friendly at all. I guess that's why they call jealousy the green-eyed monster.

You can help Jessica by making sure she knows that you like her even if you do hang out with Lori sometimes. Good friends might feel a little jealous now and then, but then they remember it's great to have lots of good friends. Jessica just needs a reminder of this.

Maybe Jessica is just feeling left out. Have you asked Jessica to join in when you and Lori are playing? That might do the trick. A lot of things are more fun with three people, like jumping rope.

Tell Jessica you want to be friends with her *and* Lori. Let her know you hope that will be OK because you'd hate to lose her friendship. When Jessica hears that, she might feel better and get over being jealous.

Tina

Dear Tina,

My best friend, Tracy, is moving away. She likes the same books I do. We talk every day after school. She sleeps over all the time. I'll really miss her, and she is really sad about moving. I know friends should help each other. How can I help Tracy?

Amber

Dear Amber,

Tracy sounds like a great best friend—the kind you'll really miss. You sound like a great friend, too, because you are thinking more about Tracy than yourself.

You and Tracy can make some plans that will help you both feel better. If it's OK with your parents, pick one night a week to call each other. Send each other e-mails and real letters. Spend a little of your money on a cool going-away present for Tracy. You could buy her some special stationery for writing to you or a cute little address book.

If Tracy isn't moving too far away, see if your mom or dad can take you two to a movie now and then. Tell Tracy how much you'll miss her and to keep in touch.

Tina

19

Dear Mica,

What a cool thing to want to do! Yes, you can make friends with kids who live far, far away—and without running up the long distance phone bill! You can be a pen pal. Pen pals write letters back and forth to each other, either through the mail or over the Internet.

There are many special pen pal groups just for kids. Have your mom, dad, or guardian sit down with you and try to find a few of these Web sites. Once you find a good site, let your parents see the letters you are writing to your new pen pal.

You could also ask your teacher to help you. Tell him about a great new project you want to start. Your whole class could get involved! It would be a great way to practice your writing skills and meet new people. You may even get some extra credit—which is always a bonus.

Tina

Dear Tina,

My friend Nathan invited me to his birthday party. That's great, but I never know what to do at a party. Who do I talk to? What if no one talks to me?

Joe

Dear Joe,

Great questions! Don't worry, Joe. Everyone gets a little scared walking into a party—even grown-ups.

Everyone at a party is a little nervous, just like you. So instead of standing there feeling nervous and wishing someone would talk to you, walk across the room and talk to another guest. See that guy standing in the corner all by himself? Walk on over, and say hello. You'll make him feel better and make yourself feel better, too.

Now, go say hello to the host. The host is the person who invited you. Find him, and let him know you're there. If you see Nathan's mom or dad, say hello to them, too. It's the polite thing to do, and it also gives you something to do for a few minutes.

Then head for the goodies! Talk to someone about the food or the pile of presents. If you find a kid you've never seen before, ask him how he knows Nathan. He might play on Nathan's hockey team and have some great stories to tell.

Think of it this way: You like Nathan and so does everyone in the room, so you'll probably like these other kids, too!

Tina

Dear Tina,

I asked Megan to sleep over, and she said no. The next day, I found out that Megan spent the night at Teresa's house. I was so mad! Maybe I shouldn't be Megan's or Teresa's friend anymore.

Ashley

24

Dear Ashley,

I don't know about you, but I don't want just one friend. I like having lots!

Think about how many friends you have and how each one is special to you. It's the same for Megan and Teresa. They probably didn't mean to hurt your feelings. Megan might have known you would be upset, so she didn't tell you she was hanging out with Teresa.

Something like that happened to me once. I felt so sad and left out when Josie and Kathy didn't ask me to go to the mall with them. Then my stepmom had a great idea. She said she'd drive us all to the mall the next weekend. We went together and had a great time. We still like our one-on-one time, too.

Talk to your parents. Maybe you can invite both girls for a slumber party next weekend! Three people doesn't have to be a crowd, it can be a small party. Have fun!

Tina

Dear Tina,

This kid, Scott, hangs around me and my friends all the time. We don't really know him, but he won't go away. Should I just tell him to get lost?

Eric

Dear Eric,

Sounds to me like Scott might be lonely and looking for some new friends.

Maybe he's a kid you'd like as a friend, maybe not. Either way, I wouldn't tell him to get lost. That's pretty rude! Why not invite Scott to play with you guys one afternoon and see how it goes? Scott may not become your very best friend, but he might be a fun guy to have on your basketball team or a nice kid to hang out with now and then.

You may not be Scott's idea of his very best friend, either. You must admire that he's brave enough to try to get to know some new kids. Introduce Scott to your buddies and to anyone else you know. You might help him find a great new friend!

Tina

27

It's Quiz Time

Grab a piece of paper and a pencil, and take this fun quiz. I won't grade you, so don't be nervous.

1. When you're the new kid at school:
   - A. tell everyone the school is dumb.
   - B. tell everyone you are so cool, and they're not.
   - C. say hi and tell everyone your name.

2. Popular kids:
   - A. never feel shy.
   - B. like to make friends just like everyone else does.
   - C. never get scared.

3. When you fight with a friend, you should:
   - A. never make up, so don't even try.
   - B. tell other kids that you won.
   - C. say you're sorry, and try to be friends again.

4. Being bossy and selfish will:
   - A. make your friends angry with you.
   - B. make your dog like you more.
   - C. get you lots of friends.

5. When your friend makes a mistake:
   - A. ask him if it would help to talk about it.
   - B. stop being his friend.
   - C. pretend you don't remember his name.

6. The maximum number of friends you can have is:
    A. one.
    B. two.
    C. as many as you want!

7. When the new kid wants to talk to you:
    A. scream and run away as fast as you can.
    B. give him a chance. You might make a new friend.
    C. pretend you don't hear him.

8. When a friend moves away, you should:
    A. forget about her.
    B. pout.
    C. wish her luck, and keep in touch.

9. You're being friendly at a party when you:
    A. sit alone, and refuse to talk.
    B. put fake bugs in the punch.
    C. talk to friends and new people.

10. If your friends have fun without you:
    A. stop being their friend.
    B. think of something fun you can all do together.
    C. have a party and don't invite them.

Answer Key: 1-C, 2-B, 3-C, 4-A, 5-A, 6-C, 7-B, 8-C, 9-C, 10-B

29

The friendliest guy I can think of is Mister Rogers. I'm sure you know him. Mister Rogers had a first name, Fred, and he wasn't just a TV star. He was a real person.

Mister Rogers was born in Pennsylvania. He studied music in college. One of his first jobs was as a puppeteer. In 1963, Mister Rogers became a minister, but he didn't work in a church. He used what he learned to work with children and families through television.

Mister Rogers' Neighborhood was on TV for almost 35 years and won many awards. One of Mister Rogers' sweaters hangs in a Smithsonian museum in Washington, D.C. How would you like to be so well-known for being friendly that your clothes were put in a museum?

The people who worked on the TV show with Mister Rogers said he really was a kind person. Mister Rogers died in 2003. He was 74. Mister Rogers once said, "I have really never considered myself a TV star. I always thought I was a neighbor who just came in for a visit."

Mister Rogers' neighborhood was such a friendly place. He taught people that love and respect are a part of every friendship. He was a great friend to millions of people.

Glossary

Here are some of my favorite words and expressions from today's letters.

advice–suggestions from people who think they know what you should do about a problem

apology–saying "I'm sorry"; sometimes it's hard to do, but it usually makes you feel better

appreciation–showing and telling friends, teachers, and other people that you notice what is special and great about them

jealousy–feeling angry and sad that your friend has another friend, or maybe he or she has a toy you'd like to have

popular–kids who look cool, have lots of friends, and don't get in trouble with their teachers; popular just means a person is well-liked

thoughtful–thinking of what your friend, your parents, or even your brother wants and needs right now

To Learn More

At the Library

Rogers, Fred. *The World According to Mister Rogers: Important Things to Remember*. New York: Hyperion, 2003.

Minarik, Else Holmelund. *Little Bear's New Friend*. New York: HarperCollins, 2002.

Nettleton, Pamela Hill. *Pocahontas: Peacemaker and Friend to the Colonists*. Minneapolis: Picture Window Books, 2004.

On the Web

FactHound offers a safe, fun way to find Web sites related to this book. All of the sites on FactHound have been researched by our staff. *www.facthound.com*

1. Visit the FactHound home page.

2. Enter a search word related to this book, or type in this special code: 1404806237.

3. Click on the FETCH IT button.

Your trusty FactHound will fetch the best Web sites for you!

Index

Books in This Series

- Do I Have To? Kids Talk About Responsibility

- How Could You? Kids Talk About Trust

- I Can Do It! Kids Talk About Courage

- Is That True? Kids Talk About Honesty

- Let's Get Along! Kids Talk About Tolerance

- May I Help You? Kids Talk About Caring

- No Fair! Kids Talk About Fairness

- Pitch In! Kids Talk About Cooperation

- Treat Me Right! Kids Talk About Respect

- Want to Play? Kids Talk About Friendliness

- We Live Here Too! Kids Talk About Good Citizenship

- You First! Kids Talk About Consideration